CONTENTS

TIPS TO COOKS

1) Read the safety rules on the opposite page and follow them. Remember: Do not cook unless your mother or another adult is with you.

2) Before you start to cook: Wash your hands, put on an apron, roll up long sleeves, and tie back long hair. Read the recipe through and ask about anything you don't understand. Get out all ingredients and equipment you will need.

3) Have your mother operate any electrical appliances.

4) Turn pot handles away from front of stove. Use pot holders to move or lift hot pots, pans, and pot lids.

5) Lift lids carefully so you don't get a face full of steam. Have your mother carry hot pots from stove and drain vegetables for you.

6) Clean up the kitchen when you have finished cooking.

WARNING

Stoves, knives and other cooking equipment can be dangerous. Always follow these safety rules to avoid painful accidents when you cook:

Have your mother light the oven or burner and set it at the temperature called for in the recipe. Do NOT cook unless your mother or some other adult is with you to help if needed.

Remember, hot grease and sugar mixtures burn easily, so burner flame should be just high enough to cook them. Watch constantly. Do NOT lean over the pan. And tie back long hair!

Using knives: Cut food with sharp edge of knife and cut away from hand holding the food. Slice and cut on a level cutting board.

SNOOPY'S STEAK TARTAR

(For DOGS only and maybe cats)

1 lb. ground pet meat
1 raw egg
dash of salt

Combine all ingredients in a small bowl and mix thoroughly. Don't count on leftovers.

GUESS WHAT, SNOOPY...

I DID SOMETHING THAT WILL HELP MAKE YOUR FUR SHINY...

I MIXED A RAW EGG IN WITH YOUR DOG FOOD

I FEEL SICK!
SCHULZ

ICING

1 cup confectioner's sugar
1½ tablespoons very soft butter
1 teaspoon vanilla or orange flavoring
dash of salt
1 cake unfrosted from the store

Blend sugar, a little at a time, with the butter. Add dash of salt. When the sugar and butter are thoroughly mixed, blend in vanilla or orange flavoring. Add a few drops of milk if icing seems very dry. It should not be runny, but smooth and soft enough to spread. Pour onto top of cake and spread lightly over the cake with a table knife or spatula.

COME ON, TRY IT... IF YOU DON'T HAVE THE CASH, YOU CAN PUT IT ON YOUR CREDIT CARD...
GOOP 5¢

GOOP 5¢

YOU WOULDN'T KNOW GOOD GOOP IF YOU TASTED IT !!!
SCHULZ

BEETHOVEN'S GREEN BEANS WITH BACON

1 lb. green beans
1 strip bacon
½ small onion, peeled
½ to ¾ teaspoon salt
2 cups water

Wash beans and cut off ends. Cut into 1 inch diagonal pieces. Place in saucepan. Add all other ingredients. Cover and boil gently until beans are tender. Drain, remove bacon and onion, and serve.

4 to 6 servings.

I NEED A GOOD PLACE TO HIDE THIS BONE..

I HATE TO BURY IT BECAUSE SOME STUPID ST. BERNARD OR SOMETHING MIGHT FIND IT...

SCHULZ
KLUNK!

I GET THE HINT!
SCHULZ

NOW I'M TOO TIRED TO EAT!
SCHULZ

HAPPINESS IS A HOT CHEESE-TOMATO SANDWICH

Cover a slice of white bread with Cheddar cheese (not too thick). Add a large slice of tomato. On top of this put 1 teaspoonful of chopped onion and 1 teaspoonful of sweet, green pickle relish. Cover with a slice of bacon that has been cut in half. Broil (do not pre-heat broiler) until bacon is done. Serve immediately.

I FEEL GUILTY ABOUT THE WAY I FEED SNOOPY...HIS MEALS ARE SO DRAB...

I SHOULD DO SOMETHING TO MAKE HIS MEALS MORE INTERESTING..

SCHULZ

PEPPERMINT PATTY'S PRUNE WHIP

1 lb. package dried prunes
water to cover
1/3 cup sugar
1/2 pint whipping cream
sugar to taste
1/2 teaspoon vanilla

Soak prunes for at least an hour in the water. Add 1/3 cup sugar, bring to a boil, and simmer (covered) for about an hour or until prunes are puffy and tender. Cool. Cut each prune in quarters, removing seeds. Chill in refrigerator. Beat cream until it begins to thicken, and add 1/2 to 1 teaspoon sugar and the vanilla. Fold in chilled prunes. Serves 6.

GOOP 5¢

I'LL TAKE A BOWL, PLEASE..

THAT'S PRETTY GOOD GOOP
THANK YOU..

ACTUALLY, IT WAS ONLY FAIR, BUT WHERE ELSE CAN YOU GET A BOWL OF GOOP FOR 5¢ ?
SCHULZ

LUCY'S LEMONADE

4 lemons
3/4 cup granulated sugar
3 tablespoons corn syrup
1 cup hot water
4 cups cold water
ice cubes
1 small bottle ginger ale
maraschino cherries

Heat hot water, sugar and syrup in saucepan over low flame, stirring until sugar is dissolved. Let cool. Wash and cut lemons in half and squeeze in lemon squeezer. Add lemon juice to cooled sugar mixture and stir. Remove any floating seeds with teaspoon. Pour lemon mixture over 8 ice cubes in a 2-quart pitcher, and add the cold water. Chill in refrigerator. Just before you serve, add ginger ale and stir. In each glass put 3 ice cubes and a cherry and fill with lemonade. Serves 6 people.

THAT ONE LOOKS LIKE A CREAM BUT YOU NEVER KNOW...THAT ONE COULD BE A CARAMEL...THERE'S NO DIVINITY, IS THERE? THAT ONE IS PROBABLY COCONUT...

THE LIGHT COLORED ONES ARE USUALLY GOOD ALTHOUGH THE DARK COLORED ONES ARE SOMETIMES CREAMS...I DON'T KNOW ABOUT THOSE SQUARE ONES...I WONDER IF..

TAKE ONE

COCONUT!
SCHULZ

YOU KNOW WHAT I HAVE IN HERE?

A DOZEN DOUGHNUTS!

JUST TO SHOW YOU MY HEART'S IN THE RIGHT PLACE, I'M GOING TO GIVE YOU ONE..

VERY FUNNY!
SCHULZ

ONE OF BEETHOVEN'S FAVORITE DISHES WAS MACARONI AND CHEESE

THE GIRL I MARRY MUST BE ABLE TO MAKE GOOD MACARONI AND CHEESE..

HOW DID BEETHOVEN FEEL ABOUT COLD CEREAL?
SCHULZ

FRANKLIN'S JAM TARTS

2 cups flour
½ teaspoon salt
⅔ to 1 cup vegetable shortening
¼ to ½ cup ice water
any kind of jam

Sift flour and salt together in a large bowl. Work shortening into flour with fingertips (be gentle) until ingredients are well blended and no large lumps of shortening remain. Dribble in enough ice water to make dough hold together in a ball—but do not make dough sticky. Roll with rolling pin into ⅛ inch thickness on a floured board. Cut dough into rounds with cookie cutter or drinking glass. Place ½ to 1 teaspoon of any kind of jam in the center of each round. Fold over into a half moon and pinch the edges together. Prick top with a fork. Bake close together on cookie sheet until golden brown on top (375°). Makes 18 to 20 tarts. Sprinkle lightly with sugar before baking, for added sweetness.

IF I WERE A WILD ANIMAL, I'D HAVE TO STALK MY SUPPER..

I'D SNEAK THROUGH THE TALL GRASS LIKE THIS.... THEN I'D..

POUNCE!

OOOO...WHAT A MESS!
SCHULZ

CHARLIE BROWN'S MOTHER'S BUTTERED OVEN-POTATOES

4 medium potatoes, peeled
½ stick butter
ice water
salt and pepper

Slice potatoes into lengths (like French fries). Soak for 1 hour in ice water. Remove and dry with paper towel. Dip each piece of potato into the melted butter and arrange in a shallow baking pan. Salt lightly with salt shaker. Cook in 375°-400° oven until potatoes are brown and tender when poked with long fork. Serves 6.

I THOUGHT YOU WERE GOING TO GET OVER YOUR BROKEN ROMANCE EASILY, BUT YOU'RE NOT, ARE YOU?

YOU'VE BEEN MOPING AROUND ALL WEEK-END....YOU'LL DESTROY YOURSELF...YOU'VE GOT TO FIND SOME WAY TO FORGET HER!

ALL RIGHT... I'LL FORGET HER THE ONLY WAY I KNOW HOW...

EATING!!
SCHULZ

CARROTS EVERYBODY LIKES

4 cups carrots, peeled and coarsely grated
½ teaspoon salt
1 teaspoon granulated sugar
1½ cups water
2 teaspoons brown sugar
¼ cup heavy cream

Cook carrots in water with salt and granulated sugar until tender. Watch carefully so that water does not cook away too fast and carrots burn.

Remove from heat and mash with potato masher (not too smooth). Add brown sugar and cream. Mix well and serve with butter on top. Serves 4.

PERHAPS I WAS A BIT TOO OBVIOUS!
SCHULZ

WHAT ARE YOU HANGING AROUND HERE FOR? IT'S NOT SUPPERTIME YET!

SIGH

MY STOMACH-CLOCK MUST BE FAST..
SCHULZ

WELL, I HOPE YOU'RE SATISFIED!

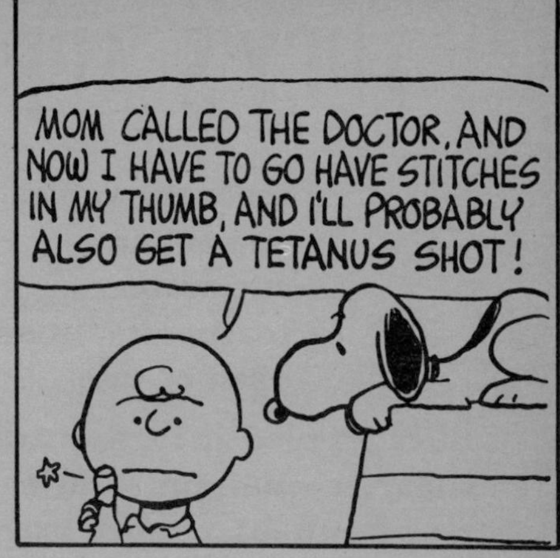
MOM CALLED THE DOCTOR, AND NOW I HAVE TO GO HAVE STITCHES IN MY THUMB, AND I'LL PROBABLY ALSO GET A TETANUS SHOT!

ALL BECAUSE I CUT MY THUMB OPENING A CAN OF DOG FOOD FOR **YOUR** SUPPER!

I'LL NEVER EAT AGAIN!
SCHULZ

LUCY'S APPLESAUCE PIE

5 medium apples, peeled and cored
½ cup sugar
¼ cup water
½ teaspoon cinnamon
dash of salt

Slice apples into a medium saucepan. Add water, sugar, cinnamon, and salt. Cook (covered and stirring frequently) until extra water is gone—being careful not to burn the apples. Stir and mash until most lumps are gone. Turn apples into an 8-inch glass pie plate and cover with a topping made of the following:

1 cup flour
6 tablespoons soft butter
½ cup (scant) brown sugar
dash of cinnamon

Blend these ingredients together with your fingertips and sprinkle over the applesauce. Bake at 375° until top is brown and crusty. Serve warm with whipped cream or vanilla ice cream. Serves 6 generously.

LOOK, IF YOU'RE GOING TO MAKE US SOME HOT CHOCOLATE, MAKE IT RIGHT!

WELL, I WAS GOING TO USE THIS BOX OF CHOCOLATE-MIX HERE, BUT I CHANGED MY MIND..

I DIDN'T WANT TO USE THIS AFTER WHAT I READ ON THE SIDE..
WHAT DOES IT SAY ON THE SIDE?

IT'S FULL OF INGREDIENTS!
SCHULZ

GREAT PUMPKIN COOKIES

1½ cups brown sugar, packed
½ cup shortening
2 eggs
1 lb. can pumpkin
2¾ cups flour, sifted
1 tablespoon baking powder
1 teaspoon cinnamon
½ teaspoon nutmeg
½ teaspoon salt
¼ teaspoon ginger
1 cup raisins
1 cup pecans, chopped

Pre-heat oven to 400°. Mix sugar, shortening, eggs, and pumpkin thoroughly in a large bowl. Sift dry ingredients and add to pumpkin mixture. Blend well. Add raisins and pecans. Drop batter by teaspoonsful on ungreased baking sheets. Bake 12 to 15 minutes or until lightly browned. Remove from oven, and lift off with a pancake turner. Makes about 6 dozen. A delicious snack while you're waiting for the "Great Pumpkin."

YOU AND SNOOPY MUST BE TIRED AND HUNGRY FROM YOUR LONG WALK..

BEFORE YOU START TO TELL ME ABOUT THE "GREAT PUMPKIN," I'LL GET US SOME MILK TO DRINK

LAP! SLURP! LAP!
SLURP! LAP!
LAP!

I GUESS I'VE SAID THIS BEFORE BUT HE'S JUST ABOUT THE MOST PECULIAR KID I'VE EVER SEEN!
Z
SCHULZ

SCHROEDER'S CHOCOLATE SAUCE

- 2 squares unsweetened chocolate (use semi-sweet if you like it sweeter)
- ½ cup honey
- 1 cup evaporated milk
- ½ teaspoon vanilla
- ½ teaspoon butter

Melt chocolate in small saucepan over larger pan of boiling water. When chocolate is melted, remove saucepan from fire and add honey and evaporated milk. Mix with a rotary beater until well blended and slightly thick. Add vanilla and butter. Store in covered jar in refrigerator.

HOW ABOUT GETTING ME A DISH OF ICE CREAM?

WELL, HURRY UP!

WHERE'S MY ICE CREAM?

SHE HAS ALL THE PATIENCE OF A BOILING TEA KETTLE..
SCHULZ

HOW ABOUT THAT?

EVERYONE IS EATING TURKEY TODAY, BUT JUST BECAUSE I'M A DOG, I GET DOG FOOD

OF COURSE, IT MIGHT HAVE BEEN WORSE...

I COULD HAVE BEEN BORN A TURKEY!
SCHULZ

Z

OH, COME NOW! LET'S NOT GET RIDICULOUS!
SCHULZ

EVERYBODY'S CHOCOLATE SODA

2 large scoops marble fudge ice cream
2 to 3 tablespoons chocolate sauce
bottle of club soda or cola

Mix one scoop of ice cream with the chocolate sauce in bottom of tall glass. Fill with soda or cola to 1 inch from the top. Stir gently and add final scoop of ice cream.

WHAT ARE YOU DOING, CHARLIE BROWN?

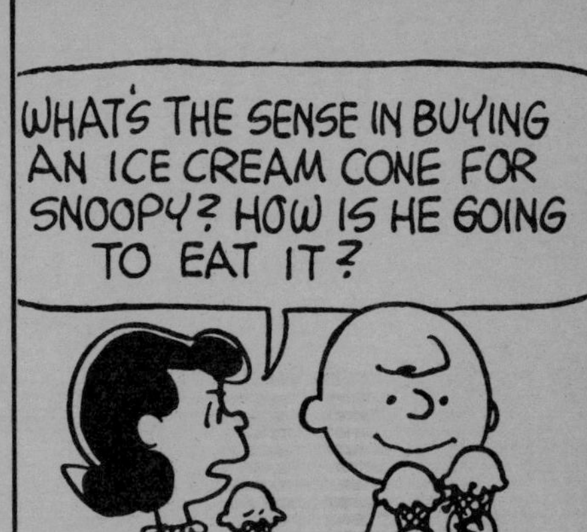
WHAT'S THE SENSE IN BUYING AN ICE CREAM CONE FOR SNOOPY? HOW IS HE GOING TO EAT IT?

HE CAN'T **HOLD** IT!

YOU DON'T HOLD AN ICE CREAM CONE...YOU TEE IT UP!
SCHULZ

SECURITY CINNAMON TOAST

8 slices white bread
½ stick (½ cube) butter
6 tablespoons granulated sugar
1 scant tablespoon cinnamon

Melt butter with sugar and cinnamon. Cook gently while toasting bread on ONE side only in broiler. Spread untoasted side of bread with sugar mixture and place under medium-hot broiler until sugar is crusty and bubbly. The sugar's hot! Be careful!

Another way Linus does it is make toast in toaster. Then he spreads it with butter immediately, and shakes a spoonful of cinnamon sugar (2 tablespoons sugar mixed with a teaspoon of cinnamon) over the buttered toast.

YOU GONNA MAKE SOME TOAST? HOW ABOUT PUTTING IN A SLICE FOR ME?

HERE YOU ARE...
THANK YOU VERY MUCH

HEY! THIS IS TOO LIGHT! IT'S HARDLY SINGED!

SURELY YOU DON'T EXPECT ME TO EAT **RAW TOAST**?!
SCHULZ

SALLY'S SCRAMBLED EGGS WITH (OR WITHOUT) STEWED TOMATOES

6 eggs
4 tablespoons milk, half and half, or cream
½ teaspoon salt
2 or 3 shakes of pepper
1 lb. can stewed tomatoes

Beat eggs in bowl until light and fluffy (a good beating makes lighter eggs). Add milk and seasoning. Cook in moderately hot pan which has been lightly buttered. Stir eggs with fork to keep from sticking and browning. Serve and top with hot, stewed tomatoes. For 4 to 6.

HERE'S "BEAU" SNOOPY OF THE FOREIGN LEGION MARCHING ACROSS THE DESERT

NOTHING BUT SAND AS FAR AS THE EYE CAN SEE...BUZZARDS CIRCLE OVERHEAD...WATER! WE MUST HAVE WATER! WATER...

HERE...YOU LOOKED KIND OF THIRSTY SO I BROUGHT YOU YOUR DISH

WHAT FUN IS THAT?

MY GRANDMOTHER USED TO PUT PEPPER AND CHILI-POWDER ON HER KIDS' THUMBS TO KEEP THEM FROM SUCKING THEM..

WHAT DO YOU THINK OF THAT IDEA?

TERRIBLE!

ALL THAT SPICY FOOD IS VERY BAD FOR YOUR STOMACH
SCHULZ

DOGS EAT GRASS, DON'T THEY?

OH, YES... I DON'T KNOW WHY, BUT THEY DO...

HEY WAKE UP! I'VE GOT SOMETHING FOR YOU..

JUST WHAT I'VE ALWAYS WANTED...A BOWL OF GRASS!
SCHULZ

FRIEDA'S FRENCH TOAST

4 slices bread (not too fresh)
2 eggs
1/3 cup milk
1 teaspoon sugar
1/8 teaspoon salt

Beat eggs until light and frothy. Add milk, sugar, and salt, and beat until well blended. Pour into wide shallow bowl. Dip each piece of bread into egg mixture and fry in medium hot pan, greased with butter, over low flame. When toast is brown on both sides and puffy, it is ready to serve. Top with melted butter and cinnamon sugar, syrup, or powdered sugar.

THE ONLY WAY TO BEAT THE COLD WEATHER IS TO HIBERNATE..

I WILL NOW SETTLE DOWN IN MY DEN, AND NOT COME OUT UNTIL....

SUPPERTIME!
SCHULZ

DIVINE DIVINITY

2 cups sugar
½ cup light corn syrup
½ cup water
2 egg whites, beaten stiff
⅛ teaspoon salt
1 teaspoon vanilla
1 cup walnuts, coarsely chopped

Cook sugar, syrup, and water, stirring until sugar dissolves. Reduce heat and cook, without stirring, until drop of syrup put into cold water forms a hard ball. Meanwhile, beat egg whites in bowl with salt until stiff. Slowly pour the hot syrup into egg whites, beating constantly with electric or hand beater. Add vanilla and nuts. Continue to beat until stiff. Drop from a teaspoon onto waxed paper. For variation, add chopped candied cherries or dates with or without the nuts.

JUST A MINUTE! HOLD EVERYTHING!

SAY, "OH, DEAR SISTER, WITH THE SWEET FACE AND BEAUTIFUL SMILE, MAY I HAVE A PIECE OF DIVINITY?"

OH, DEAR SISTER, WITH THE SWEET FACE AND BEAUTIFUL SMILE, MAY I HAVE A PIECE OF DIVINITY?

FOR DIVINITY I'LL SAY ANYTHING, NO MATTER HOW NAUSEATING!!
SCHULZ

SALLY'S BROILED CHEESE HOT-DOG SANDWICH

10 hot dogs
5 hamburger buns
½ lb. Jack or Swiss Cheese

Place hot dogs in broiler. While they are browning, halve and butter hamburger buns. When hot dogs are done, remove and split lengthwise. Then cut these two pieces across in half. Arrange the four pieces on buttered bun and cover with a ¼-inch slice of cheese. Return to broiler and cook slowly until cheese is bubbly. Serve with relish, mustard, catsup, etc. Makes 10 open sandwiches.

SUPPERTIME!

GOOD GRIEF!
SCHULZ

BLEAH!

WHAT IN THE WORLD **ARE** THOSE?

SOUR MARSHMALLOWS!
SCHULZ

!

THAT'S THE LAST STRAW! IF HE WANTS ANY SUPPER, HE CAN COME AND GET IT HIMSELF!

SERVANTS' ENTRANCE IN THE REAR

LINUS' LEMON-PINEAPPLE-CARROT SALAD

1 package lemon-flavored gelatin (containing sugar)
1 13½ oz. can crushed pineapple
water
2 medium carrots, grated fine

Shake package of gelatin into bowl and pour over it 1 cup boiling water. Stir until gelatin is dissolved. Add ½ cup cold water. Stir pineapple (undrained) and grated carrots into gelatin. Pour into single or individual molds. Set in refrigerator to harden. Serve on lettuce with dollop of mayonnaise.

Serves 4 to 6.

AH! HERE COMES THE WAITER WITH MY MEAL!

I MUST THINK OF SOME NICE WAY TO SHOW MY APPRECIATION..

SMAK

THAT WASN'T IT!
SCHULZ

LUCY'S LEMON SQUARES

1 cup flour
½ cup butter
¼ cup powdered sugar

Sift flour and sugar into bowl. Blend in butter with clean fingertips until well mixed. Pat evenly into the bottom of an 8 x 8 inch baking pan. Bake for 20 minutes at 350°. Meanwhile, beat together:

2 eggs
1 cup granulated sugar
½ teaspoon baking powder
2½ tablespoons fresh lemon juice
dash of salt

Pour over baked crust and return to oven for 20-25 minutes at same temperature.

Cool on rack. Cut in squares. Sprinkle with sifted, powdered sugar.

AHEM!

OH, IS IT TIME FOR YOUR AFTERNOON SNACK?

WELL, IN THAT CASE, I'LL TELL THE OTHER TEAM TO GO ON HOME, AND I'LL TELL EVERYONE ON OUR TEAM TO GO ON HOME, AND WE'LL JUST CALL THIS GAME OFF RIGHT IN THE MIDDLE OF THE FOURTH INNING, AND GO FIX YOUR LITTLE SNACK

HOW SARCASTIC CAN YOU GET?
SCHULZ

RED BARON ROOT BEER

Fill an ice tray with root beer. Add one maraschino cherry (with stem) to each ice cube section. Freeze. Pour more root beer into glasses. Drop 2 frozen root-beer cubes into each glass. Serve at once.

HERE'S THE WORLD WAR I FLYING ACE WALKING ONTO THE FIELD.."GOOD MORNING, CHAPS!" (THESE ARE GOOD LADS)

BUT WHAT'S THIS? THERE'S EXCITEMENT AMONG THE ENLISTED MEN... SOME SORT OF RUMOR GOING ABOUT..

HERE'S THE FLYING ACE REPORTING TO HIS COMMANDING OFFICER... "GOOD MORNING, SIR..A ROOT BEER? YES, SIR, I DON'T MIND IF I DO"

THERE MUST BE SOMETHING BIG COMING UP... HE ONLY OFFERS ME A ROOT BEER WHEN THERE'S A DANGEROUS MISSION TO BE FLOWN!
SCHULZ

HERE YOU ARE, SNOOPY...HAPPY THANKSGIVING!

THANK YOU

NO CRANBERRIES ?
SCHULZ

HEY, MANAGER, I HAVE A REQUEST..

TRY TO PITCH SO THAT NO ONE HITS ME A FLY BALL THIS INNING...I DON'T HAVE ANY ROOM IN MY GLOVE FOR A FLY BALL...

WHAT'S THAT YOU HAVE IN IT ?

RICE CUSTARD!
SCHULZ

HERE YOU ARE, SNOOPY... SUPPERTIME!

THAT'S FUNNY...MOST WAITERS **LIKE** TO HAVE THEIR CUSTOMERS BE ENTHUSIASTIC!
SCHULZ

FEED THE DOG! FEED THE DOG! FEED THE DOG!

AND YOU DON'T EVEN GET ANY THANKS FOR IT..

SMACK

WELL, MOST OF THE TIME YOU DON'T...
SCHULZ

SUPPERTIME!

SUPPERTIME! SUPPERTIME! SUPPERTIME! GOOD OL' SUP, SUP, SUP, SUPPERTIME!

SUPPERTIME!

I MUST ADMIT HE'S A VERY SATISFYING PERSON TO COOK FOR
SCHULZ